Teacher Gwynneth's Poetry for Children

Book 1

By Gwynneth D. Walker

Compiled By: Althea N. Martin, B.S. in Ed., M. Ed.

Illustrated By: Jody H. Darrow

This is a work of Fiction.

Ordering Information:

 BookTrail Agency
8838 Sleepy Hollow Rd.
Kansas City, MO 64114

Printed in the United States of America

Preface

Teacher Gwynneth was truly a child of God!
She imparted her love and understanding of nature
To the boys and girls through classroom activities and
Poetry. Every child who "Graduated" from her pre-
Kindergarten class was surely blessed!

a.n.m.

Table of Contents

Sing a Song of Friendship

Sing a song of friendship
Love for one another;
Dark child and white child
And oriental brother

Color doesn't matter
It's just another name;
Our Father made us one and all
And loves us all the same.

Wisdom

"What things are beautiful?"
I asked a four year old.
"Leaves when they fall", he said
"And walking when it's cold."

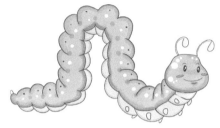

Little Caterpillar

Little caterpillar go creep, creep, creep,
Now it is time for your winter sleep;
Spin your cocoon and cuddle down inside,
Nobody knows on a twig you hide.

When the snow has melted and violets bloom,
Little Caterpillar you'll need more room;
Burst your cocoon, and open your eye,
Spread out your wings lovely butterfly.

The Squirrel

A little squirrel up in a tree,

Sat on his haunches looking at me.

"Hello", I said to the little chap,

"It's time you were taking your winter nap."

The cold north wind came whistling by,

And tumbling snowflakes whitened the sky,

But the squirrel safe in his oak-tree bed,

Just curled up his tail and tucked in his head.

Rain

Pitter, patter, pitter, patter,
Hear the raindrops silver sound;
Pitter, patter, pitter, patter,
Making puddles on the ground.

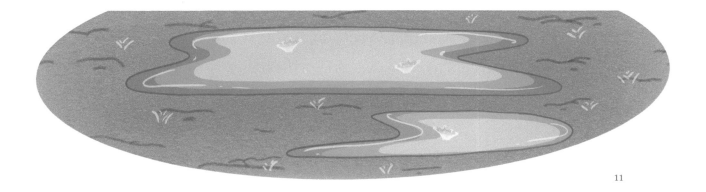

The Cardinal

The cardinal is singing
I hear his cheery note
Pouring in sweet melody
From his crimson throat.
Good cheer!
Good cheer!

He wears a little top-knot
I think it's called a crest,
And there's nothing that is redder
Than the feathers on his breast.
Good cheer!
Good cheer!

The Awakening

"Oh, goodness me!" said mother earth all to herself one day,
I think it's time for me to put my winter clothes away.
The hyacinths and daffodils have wakened from their sleep;
I cannot keep account of them, for everywhere they peep!
The pussy willows, naughty things, have taken off their caps,
And all the little crocuses have wakened from their naps.
The buds upon the maple tree are swelling full and brown,
And from reports my ear has heard the cardinal's in town!
It's time to get my brushes out and sweep the meadows clean,
And send my little shower-baths to brighten up the green.

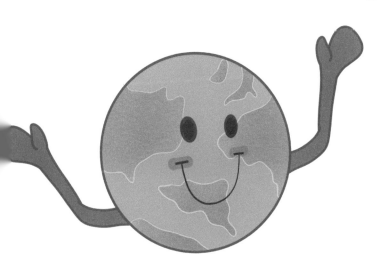

The Storm

Hear the thunder crash,

See the lightning flash!

Watch the heavy raindrops fall,

Soon the storm will pass.

Eagerly the flowers

Drink the falling rain;

See the rainbow in the sky,

It is clear again.

Lady Daffodil

Pretty lady daffodil
Wears a bonnet with a frill
And a petalled ruff of gold
To protect her from the cold.

My Shadow

Close to my feet
When the sun is out
A queer little shadow
Keeps bobbing about.

Sometimes he's fat,
And sometimes he's thin
But he's nothing at all
When the sun goes in!

Buttercups

I know that spring is here because
I hear the robins sing,
And all the little buttercups
Are dancing in a ring.

Little Green Frog

A little green frog
(Who lived 'neath the mill)
Sat on a toadstool
On top of a hill.

A butterfly bright
Flew over his head.
"I think you would do
For me!" he said

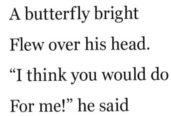

The butterfly laughed.
"Kind sir," said she,
"I may do for you,
But you wouldn't for me!"

Fish Tale

Five little fishes were swimming in a brook.
Jamie caught one and took it home to cook.
Mother and Daddy were pleased as punch;
And all the family had fish for lunch.

Modest Wee Violet

Modest, wee violet, timid and shy,

What other flower with your sweetness can vie?

Dwelling ' mid grasses and by tinkling brooks,

Hiding in all woodland corners and nooks.

Modest, wee violet, timid and shy

No other flower with your sweetness can vie!

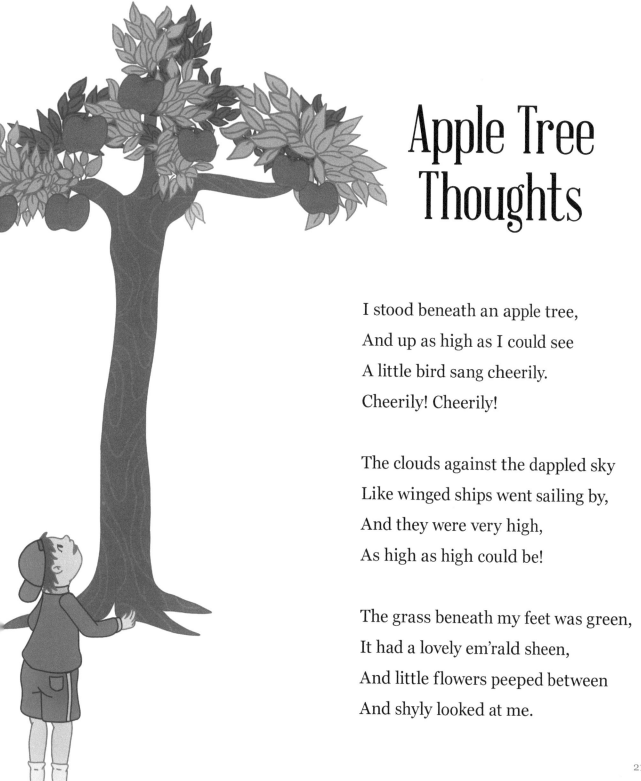

Apple Tree Thoughts

I stood beneath an apple tree,
And up as high as I could see
A little bird sang cheerily.
Cheerily! Cheerily!

The clouds against the dappled sky
Like winged ships went sailing by,
And they were very high,
As high as high could be!

The grass beneath my feet was green,
It had a lovely em'rald sheen,
And little flowers peeped between
And shyly looked at me.

The Party

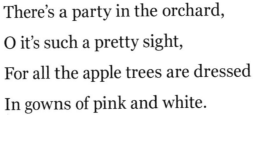

There's a party in the orchard,
O it's such a pretty sight,
For all the apple trees are dressed
In gowns of pink and white.

The birds have been invited.
They are singing in the trees,
And all the butterflies have come
And swarms of golden bees.

I think I'll join the party.
I don't believe they'd mind.
For the birds and bees and butterflies
Are really very kind.

Penguins

This is the way the penguins walk.

They cannot fly and they cannot talk.

Their wings are black and their shirts are white.

The penguin birds are a beautiful sight.

Here is something very funny –

The penguins slide on their snow white tummy!

Swinging

Up in the air and down again
I swing on a summer's day;
Now I am touching the bending grass,
Now I am far away.

Up in the air and down again
Borne by the racing breeze;
Now I am watching the clouds that sail
Over the tossing trees.

Up in the air and down again
Swift as the birds that fly;
Now I am brushing the sunlit flowers,
Now I am in the sky.

My Rockingchair Horse

O my rockingchair horse is a beautiful steed

And he has such a rollicking rock-away speed!

I climb on his back and I straddle my legs

And tuck my feet under his rockingchair pegs

And away we both go on the wings of the breeze

To a kingdom where little boys do as they please!

Raindrops

I like to hear the raindrops
When I am in my bed;
They sound like elfin footsteps
That trip above my head.

And when the house is silent
And everyone is still,
They patter, patter, patter
Against my window still.

Where Do All The Daises Go?

Where do all the daises go
When they wither up and die,
Do the fairies stooping low
Pick them to adorn the sky?

Grass

I stood knee deep
In the clover-cool grass
And laughed with delight
As I saw the wind pass.

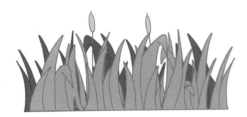

Slumber — Land

The sandman comes from slumber-land
To visit boys and girls;
He drops his star-dust in their eyes
And on their tousled curls.

He tip-toes oh so quietly
Beside each little bed,
Then smiles goodnight,
The stars are bright,
Sleep sweetly, sleepy head.

Turtle Thoughts

Under the rushes

The turtles hide

With their heads tucked in

And their tails outside.

Autumn

Today, as I watched the leaves whirling in the dance of autumn
I observed the effect it had on our Nursey School children.
It took Georgie, aged two years and five months, about fifty
seconds to become one of the leaves he had been watching.
You could tell by the glint in his eyes, the smile on his lips,
And the rhythm of his body how thoroughly he was enjoying the
experience. Leaves were such fun! Roger, aged four, unable
to become a leaf in fact, turned a wistful face to the sky and
said, "I wonder how it feels to be a leaf up there? I wonder!

The Cloudlets Party

The cloudlets had a party at the time of setting sun.

In greens and golds and rosy hues they floated one by one.

The sunbeams were the hostesses who kissed each cloudlet wee,

And for refreshments dewdrops clear were served as fairy tea.

However soon sweet Evening Star appeared and chased away.

The little cloudlets every one in party dresses gay.

But later, when the moon arose, alas what did she find!

A naughty little truant cloud that had been left behind,

Shorn of her dress of rosy hue and weeping dewy tears,

By wanton breezes cast about despite protests and fears.

Pale Lady Moon took pity on the cloudlet left to roam,

So with a dress all silver-lined she sent the truant home!

Biography

Gwynneth Dorothy Rosalind Walker was born on January 15, 1906 in Birtle, a small town, in the Province of Manitoba, Canada. She was the youngest of the seven children in this family. They were all born in England with the exception of Gwynneth.

The family moved to Brooklyn, New York, when she was one month old. Gwynneth attended a Brooklyn elementary school until the age of ten. The family then moved to Haddonfield, New Jersey, where they resided permanently.

Upon graduating from Haddonfield High School she attended the University of North Carolina for a short time. Later, Gwynneth enrolled in classes at the Moore Institute of Art in Philadelphia, Pennsylvania and took courses in Early Childhood Education at Glassboro College and at Rutgers University in New Jersey.

Gwynneth loved her work with the little children at the Haddonfield Friends School where she taught until her death. She devoted her life to the Pre-kindergarten classroom. The "Curriculum" she presented instilled a love of nature and an appreciation of language through her original poetry. She was, also, an artist who further expressed her love of nature through paintings of out-door scenery.

Although she passed away in 1964 at the age of fifty-eight years, Gwynneth has left a legacy to all boys and girls through her poetry. The verses are ageless in their appeal and, hopefully, will be enjoyed by future generations of your children.

a.n.m

Althea N. Martin, a dedicated school psychologist, was very impressed with Teacher Gwynneth D. Walker when her daughter attended Haddonfield Friends School pre-kindergarten class. Every year a "Spring Frolic" was held in May where each class presented a sketch or activity in tribute to Spring. One year Teacher Gwynneth had each child in her class dress as a flower and little Althea was a white rose.

Upon the untimely death of Gwynneth D. Walker, Althea, Sr. recognized the value of the poetry and songs that Gwynneth had created. She felt that they should not be lost and was granted permission by the Walker family to compile and copyright her material.

The seven books, compiled from Teacher Gwynneth's work, have been enhanced with the illustrations by Jody H. Darrow. Althea, Sr. searched for many years before this dream was finally realized.

May the words, music and thoughts created by Teacher Gwynneth live on for future children and adults to enjoy. All who love nature's beauty, poetry, and songs will be blessed to have the legacy of Gwyneth D. Walker touch their lives.

Jody H. Darrow's artistic gift from God was first recognized when she was a child by her father; a master printer and owner of the Hibbert Printing Co. of Trenton, NJ. The business was lost during the "Great Depression." Several years later her father passed away.

Lack of finances prevented any further education for Jody but her love of art and talent kept her actively interested in drawing. Through the years she illustrated catalogs, posters, murals, books and stories at an amateur level. Humbly, she believed that her lack of formal education limited her horizons.

Jody's public relations positions at the Washington Crossing Foundation gave her the opportunity to be considered semi-professional. When Althea N. Martin asked her to do the illustrations for the books by Gwynneth D. Walker, Jody felt she attained a professional level.

The illustrations, undoubtedly, have enhanced the wonderful verses of the books and will entertain children and adults for many years.

Addendum

The following books were also written by:

GWYNNETH D. WALKER

1. Poetry for Children – Book II
2. Songs for Children
3. Astral Thoughts
4. Heartstrings
5. Astral Songs
6. Child's First School Experience (Syllabus)

CPSIA information can be obtained
at www.ICGtesting.com
Printed in the USA
LVHW072206060422
715565LV00018B/83